THIS BOOK BELONGS TO

All rights reserved
Copyright © Banji Alexander, 2025.

The right of Banji Alexander to be identified as the author of this work has been asserted in accordance with Section 78 of the Copyright, Designs and Patents Act 1988.

The book cover picture is copyright to Banji Alexander.

This book is published by
S G Lit Books
Hamilton House
4A The Avenue, Highams Park, E4 9LD
www.sglitbooks.com

This book is sold subject to the conditions that it shall not, by way of trade or otherwise, be lent, resold, hired out or otherwise circulated without the author's or publisher's prior consent in any form of binding or cover other than that in which it is published and without a similar condition including this condition being imposed on the subsequent purchaser.

No copies of any page may be made except under licence.
You cannot copy or distribute further.

A CIP record for this book
is available from the British Library

ISBN 978-1-7393525-2-3

Reflections

A Keepsake Book for Year 6 Leavers

Banji Alexander

SG Lit
www.sglitbooks.com

To my son, Poet. Daddy loves you.
Sunrise: 2024

For Grandma Siliki
Sunrise: 1928
Sunset: 2024

For Grandma Victoria
Sunrise: 1932
Sunset: 2024

For Uncle John
Sunrise: 1953
Sunset: 2024

Contents

Introduction		8 – 9
How Are You Feeling?		10 – 11
Who Can Help Me?	YOUR FIRST WEEK AT SECONDARY SCHOOL	12 – 13
Relaxation Activities	DON'T STRESS!	14 – 15
Keeping Safe	CHILD EXPLOITATION AND KNIFE CRIME	16 – 17
Keeping Safe	E-SAFETY & CYBERBULLYING	18 – 21
Friendships and Relationships	WHEN FRIENDSHIPS END	22 – 23
Friendships and Relationships	BOUNDARIES & CONSENT	24 – 25
Personal Hygiene During Puberty		26 – 29
Lunchtimes	NUTRITION	30 – 31
Growth Mindset	POSITIVE AFFIRMATIONS	32 – 33
Things I Wish I'd Known	TOP TIPS FOR STARTING SECONDARY SCHOOL	34 – 35
Ready, Set, Go!	CHECKLIST FOR STARTING SECONDARY SCHOOL	36 – 37
Signature Signing Pages		40 – 49
Yearbook		50 – 59

INTRODUCTION

Dear Year 6,

It is almost time to venture out of the nest and step into the big wide world! Time for **change**. Your time at primary school has been preparing you for this moment since Nursery/Reception Class. Growing and evolving over the years, you have learnt valuable life skills at school that will stand you in good stead.

As we follow the group of children featured in this book on their transition journeys to secondary school, I hope you are able to reflect on their experiences and that their stories offer you guidance, empowering you, so you feel more confident and prepared for starting secondary school.

I hope the yearbook feature will allow you to capture some lasting memories and photographs from primary school. Keep this book safe, you'll cherish it more in years to come!

Goodluck and be brave!
Banji =)

Reflection:

What do you like about the way things are now?

What do you miss about the way things used to be?

STICK PHOTO IN HERE

Younger Me   Date:

STICK PHOTO IN HERE

Older Me   Date:

HOW ARE YOU FEELING?

The transition from primary to secondary school is an exciting time. There will be a number of changes which may trigger mixed emotions. You may feel excited and eager for the move, or may feel quite overwhelmed and anxious, or somewhere in between. It is always helpful to talk to others about how we are feeling. You can discuss your feelings with trusted friends and adults.

You'd be surprised to find out that many of your peers are worried about similar things, so don't keep your feelings bottled in.

Maybe you are excited about learning new subjects and making new friends.

Perhaps you're worried about leaving old friends behind.

It could be you're worried about being late to school as you familiarise yourself with the new route.

Or maybe you're unsure about taking the school bus because of the older children.

All of your feelings are valid!

With a friend or an adult, discuss how you are feeling about leaving primary school and starting secondary school.

Reflection:

How are you feeling right now?

What changes are you looking forward to?

What changes are you worried about?

What changes are you unsure about?

Make some notes below and compare them with a friend. Are there any similarities?

Changes that I am looking forward to

Changes that I am worried about

Changes that I am unsure about

WHO CAN HELP ME?
YOUR FIRST WEEK AT SECONDARY SCHOOL

It's Parker's first day at secondary school. Although she has been looking forward to this day for months, she is now feeling quite worried. She could not get to sleep on time last night as she was so excited thinking about her new school. Waking up late this morning, she rushed to get ready and has since realised she forgot to pack her pencil case. The school bell is about to ring and Parker feels like crying.

Reflection:
- What things are Parker in control of?
- What things are out of her control?
- Who at secondary school can she go to for help?

There will always be help available. Do you know who to seek help from at your new school?

Using the notes made in *'How Are You Feeling?'*, let's dissect our feelings further by exploring **why** we might be worried. With a friend or trusted adult, discuss strategies and possible solutions and record them in the table below. Use the example to guide you.

Why am I worried?	Who can help me?	Strategy or Solution
I am worried about leaving old friends behind because I find it difficult to make new friends.	My form tutor (or a trusted adult) - if I am feeling anxious and need to talk to someone.	• Start a conversation with someone in my form class who I'm seated next to. • Smile, make eye contact, and be approachable. • Join a club

RELAXATION ACTIVITIES
DON'T STRESS!

It is human to feel a little worried about the new experiences that lie ahead. As discussed in earlier pages, it is always a good idea to talk to trusted individuals about how we are feeling, write our feelings down, and try and think of solutions or strategies to overcome them. Never shy away from asking an adult for help.

If you are feeling stressed, it is a good idea to do something safe and enjoyable which helps you feel calm. When you are **relaxed**, there will be more clarity and focus to deal with the things that are worrying you.

Try and timetable relaxation activities into your day. This could be at home or at school during break time.

Reflection:

When was the last time you were stressed?

What activities help you to relax when you're stressed?

What do you like to do for fun?

HOW DO YOU RELAX?

USE A STRESS RELIEF BALL.

DO BREATHING EXERCISES.

GO FOR A BIKE RIDE.

DANCE TO YOUR FAVOURITE SONGS.

READ! ESCAPE INTO THE WORLD OF LITERATURE.

SPEND SOME TIME CREATING ART.

TAKE A WALK OR GO FOR A JOG.

PLAY A SPORT.

TRY STRETCHING OR YOGA.

KEEPING SAFE

CHILD EXPLOITATION AND KNIFE CRIME

A few weeks after starting their new school, Sebastian and Jermaine were introduced to local drug dealers, T-Monie and Grizz, by some older boys after school. They were told they could make fast money delivering packages. At first, Sebastian and Jermaine were reluctant to accept the offer, but when they saw how much money they could be making, they soon changed their minds. T-Monie and Grizz also offered them new phones and protection from any rival gangs.

Reflection:

If you were in Sebastian or Jermaine's position, what would you do?

Who can Sebastian and Jermaine turn to for help?

Child Criminal Exploitation

When someone uses a child (anyone under the age of 18) to commit a crime for them, this is called child criminal exploitation.

The exploitative relationship involves a dynamic where a child receives a 'reward' for completing a criminal task for an adult (or older person). The reward can be anything: food, money, gifts, and even affection.

Many children and young people do not realise they are being exploited. They may appear as criminals, but they are also victims.

Who Can Help?

Trusted adults: teachers, school staff, youth workers, family, sports coaches

The police

Report anonymously with Fearless - 0800 555 111 www.fearless.org

Childline - 0800 1111 www.childline.org.uk

Barnardos - www.barnardos.org.uk

The Children's Society - www.childrenssociety.org.uk

Realising that many drug dealers carry weapons, Sebastian and Jermaine are starting to have second thoughts. One of their older friends, Corey, who was stabbed after a fight with local teenagers, has advised them to carry a knife for protection. Although Corey was stabbed with his own knife (after it was snatched from him), Sebastian and Jermaine still think it's a good idea to carry a weapon for protection.

Knife Crime

Children and young people who do not feel safe in their communities sometimes believe that carrying a knife is the only solution. If someone is carrying a knife, it is more than likely that in the spur of the moment, they will use it.

Carrying a weapon is illegal and can ruin the life of both the victim and the perpetrator. Children are not exempt from facing the consequences of the law.

What advice would you give to Sebastian and Jermaine? Using the speech bubble below, give them advice, including who they can go to for help.

KEEPING SAFE

E-SAFETY

There are many positive aspects to using the internet. One can gain easy access to learning resources, stay connected with family and friends via social media, and use gaming and streaming platforms for entertainment purposes.

Lola has been chatting online with 'Kevin', a boy she met on Tik-Tok, who claims to attend her new school. He has asked Lola lots of personal questions about herself and wants her to share some revealing pictures.

Catfishing

When someone creates a fake online profile to try to deceive people into forming relationships with them, this is called catfishing.

Lola is starting to become suspicious of Kevin. He keeps on finding excuses to avoid sharing any of his pictures with her, yet she has shared personal information with him and lots of her pictures, including some that make her feel uncomfortable. He is now threatening to share them with her family.

Reflection:
Lola has been catfished. She has shared personal information, including pictures, with a stranger online. What should she do?

Safety Tips!

- Be on the look out for fake online profiles. Some people pretend to be somebody else online.

- Do not speak to strangers online if you do not know them in real life.

- Think before you share, as you have no control over where things might end up.

- Remember, anything you share online, including pictures, videos, and comments, could be difficult to remove from the internet.

- Do not share personal information like your real name, date of birth, school, and your address.

- If you are being threatened online, stop responding and do not send anything they've asked for.

- Tell a trusted adult what's happening. We all make mistakes - a problem shared is a problem halved.

Cyberbullying

If you are being bullied online, you can report it on the app or website and block those doing the bullying. Do not reply to any messages or posts, and it is always a good idea to keep evidence of what is happening by taking screenshots and keeping a diary. Never keep things bottled up inside, speak to your teachers at school and trusted adults.

Who Can Help?

Trusted adults: teachers, school staff, youth workers, family, sports coaches

Childline - 0800 1111 www.childline.org.uk

Internet Watch Foundation - www.iwf.org.uk

National Bullying Helpline - 0845 22 55 787

www.nationalbullyinghelpline.co.uk

Some girls from Charlotte's new school are being unkind to her online and sending rude messages about her in a group chat she is included in.

What advice would you give to Charlotte? Using the speech bubble below, give her advice, including who she can go to for help.

FRIENDSHIPS AND RELATIONSHIPS

WHEN FRIENDSHIPS END

Friendships play an important role in our lives. They help boost our emotional wellbeing and give us a sense of belonging. True friends support us during difficult times and contribute to our happiness.

Muna and Dwight have been friends since the start of primary school. They are next door neighbours and have always enjoyed walking to school together. They are both excited to learn they will be attending the same secondary school, and have made plans to continue to walk to school together.

Reflection:

What makes a good friendship?

What are some things you have in common with your friends?

Can you think of a time when a friend cheered you up or made you feel special?

Using the notepad below, write down words to describe the qualities of a good friend.

Qualities of a Good Friend

Since starting their new school, Muna and Dwight have grown distant. Muna has made new friends with some of the girls in her form class and has started walking to school with them instead. Dwight is confused about why things have changed and feels hurt and let down by Muna.

It is normal to feel upset when friendships come to an end. We may find it confusing and struggle to manage our emotions. Moving on after losing a good friend can be challenging.

Reflection:

Why do you think some friendships come to an end?

What do you think Dwight can do to make himself feel better?

If you knew Dwight, how could you support him?

When a friendship comes to an end, emotions will always run high. Remember, time is a healer and things will get better eventually. You can always tell a trusted person how you are feeling and write down your thoughts.

Try writing your friend a goodbye letter. You will not send the letter, but it is a good way to say goodbye and reflect on the good memories that you shared.

FRIENDSHIPS AND RELATIONSHIPS

BOUNDARIES & CONSENT

Dwight is eager to make new friends. At lunchtime, he meets Penelope, who is also keen to make new friends. Penelope and Dwight have discovered they have similar interests and live two streets away from each other. Dwight suggests they should meet after school and walk home together. Penelope thinks it's a good idea.

After school, Penelope and Dwight begin the walk home together, but then things get a little awkward. Dwight playfully puts his arm around Penelope, which makes her feel uncomfortable.

Dwight is not respecting Penelope's **personal space** and has not asked for her **consent** to put his arm around her.

Setting Boundaries

It is important to set boundaries to inform others of what we are okay with and what makes us feel uncomfortable. Setting boundaries can protect us from unwanted physical touch, and anything else (physically or emotionally) that makes us feel uncomfortable. It is important to let people know when they have crossed a boundary to prevent the same behaviour from reoccurring.

Reflection:
What do you think Penelope should do?

Using the speech bubbles below, demonstrate how Dwight could have asked Penelope for her consent and how she might respond to set her boundaries.

Dwight

Penelope

PERSONAL HYGIENE DURING PUBERTY

During puberty, your body will go through a number of changes triggered by hormones. During this time, your personal hygiene practices will also need to change to care for your developing body. **Personal hygiene** is how you care for your body and keep it clean.

What Is Puberty?

Puberty is the time during which a child matures into a young adult. Over time, a child's body will gradually develop into an adult's body and both physical and emotional changes will occur. Puberty can start as early as age 8 or as late as age 16. It happens at different times for each individual.

Your body may have already started going through a number of changes, so it is important to establish daily routines to maintain good personal hygiene.

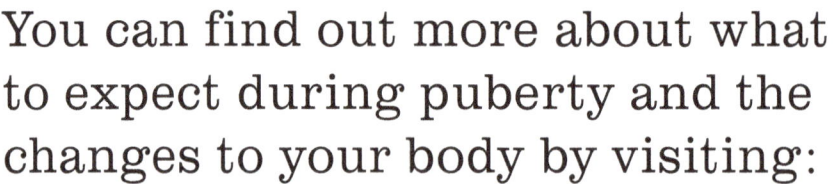

You can find out more about what to expect during puberty and the changes to your body by visiting:

www.childline.org.uk/puberty

HERE ARE SOME TIPS FOR STAYING CLEAN!

Oral Hygiene

It is important to maintain good oral hygiene to prevent bad breath, tooth decay, and gum disease. Brush your teeth twice a day, in the morning and before you go to bed. Visit the dentist regularly and avoid sugary foods and drinks.

Skincare

During puberty, your skin will produce more oil as a result of hormones which can also lead to spots. You will need to adopt a face cleansing routine, washing your face in the morning and in the evening.

Be sure to find a moisturiser that suits your skin type. You might have dry skin, oily skin, or combination skin. Drinking lots of water also helps, and remember to eat a balanced diet.

Washing Your Hair

The sebaceous glands on your scalp will produce more oil during puberty, which means you will also need to adopt a hair washing routine which works best for the type of hair you have. Some people will need to wash their hair daily to prevent it from becoming too oily and looking greasy, whereas others with different hair textures (like afro hair) may only need to wash their hair once a week, or every other week. Speak to a trusted adult who has similar hair to you, and find out what their hair routine is.

Smelly Feet

Make sure you clean your feet thoroughly when you are in the shower. Use an antibacterial soap to wash them at least once a day. Before putting on your socks and shoes, make sure your feet are completely dry – you can use a foot powder or antiperspirant. It is also a good idea to let your footwear dry out before wearing them again and do not wear the same socks two days in a row.

Nails

Keep your fingernails and toenails trimmed. Be sure to scrub out any dirt to prevent infections, and to prevent germs transferring to your mouth, eyes, and nose, from your fingernails.

Body Odour (BO)

During puberty, you will begin to sweat more as your sweat glands become activated. As bacteria breaks down the sweat on your body, body odour is produced. To avoid body odour, shower twice daily, washing your armpits and groin area with soap. As hair starts to grow in new places on your body, you may need to start shaving your armpits regularly and using antiperspirants, deodorants or a roll on. It is important you wear clean clothes every day and wash previously used clothes, as bacteria will build up on them.

Task:

At home, try and find out about a parent or guardian's personal hygiene routine.

LUNCHTIMES

NUTRITION

For many primary school pupils, the most enjoyable part of the school day is lunchtime. Although it is the most unstructured portion of the school day, it allows for pupils to improve their communication and social interaction skills by spending time with their peer group.

Great friendships have been formed during lunchtimes, and this will likely be the same at secondary school as you make new friends.

Throughout your time at primary school, your parents, guardians, and canteen staff (if you have school lunches) have made sure that you have had a balanced meal, giving you all the nutrition you need.

In secondary school, you will have more control over what you eat and will need to make healthy choices and budget your lunch money.

Visit
www.nutrition.org.uk

Reflection:

What should a balanced meal consist of?

What will you miss the most about lunchtimes at primary school?

What are you most looking forward to about lunchtimes at secondary school?

Have a look at the Eatwell plate below and try and find out about the food options available at your new school by visiting their website.

STICK PHOTO IN HERE

Lunchtime at primary school   Date:

GROWTH MINDSET
POSITIVE AFFIRMATIONS

If you have a growth mindset, you believe that anything is achievable when you work hard for it. You will be resilient and won't give up easily. People with a growth mindset understand that **making mistakes** is part of the learning journey and an opportunity to improve for next time.

Reggie is excited about starting secondary school, as he is eager to learn new subjects and new skills. He's undecided on what his dream job is for the future, but he believes that working hard and believing in himself is a good place to start.

Reggie has formed the habit of saying these **positive affirmations** to himself daily, to encourage his growth mindset:

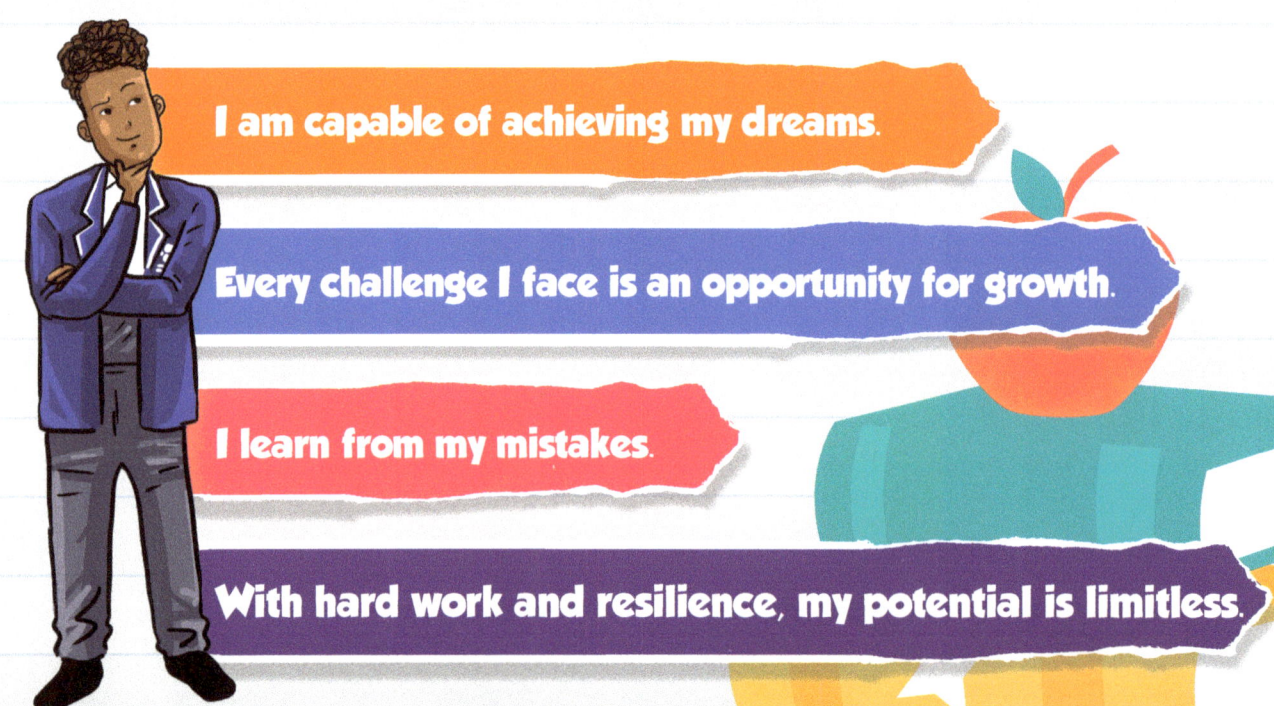

I am capable of achieving my dreams.

Every challenge I face is an opportunity for growth.

I learn from my mistakes.

With hard work and resilience, my potential is limitless.

Remember, hard work and believing in yourself will allow you to get better at just about anything and develop new skills for your future aspirations.

I am reliable! I am compassionate! I am adaptable! I am competitive!

Using the star-bursts below, write down some of your own positive affirmations.

THINGS I WISH I'D KNOWN

TOP TIPS FOR STARTING SECONDARY SCHOOL

Freddie found the start of Year 7 challenging, but eventually got into the swing of things by creating a routine for himself. Here are his top ten tips:

- Always have an open mind and be willing to try new activities and explore joining new clubs.
- Pack your bag the night before and check your timetable to ensure you have the right equipment and kit. Only pack what you need, not everything!
- Exchange numbers with some people in your class. You might need support from each other when you're at home if you're unsure about anything.
- Make sure you ask questions about your homework so you have enough information written down for when you're at home.

READY, SET, GO!

CHECKLIST FOR STARTING SECONDARY SCHOOL

☑ Tick items off your checklist over the summer break as you countdown to your first day.

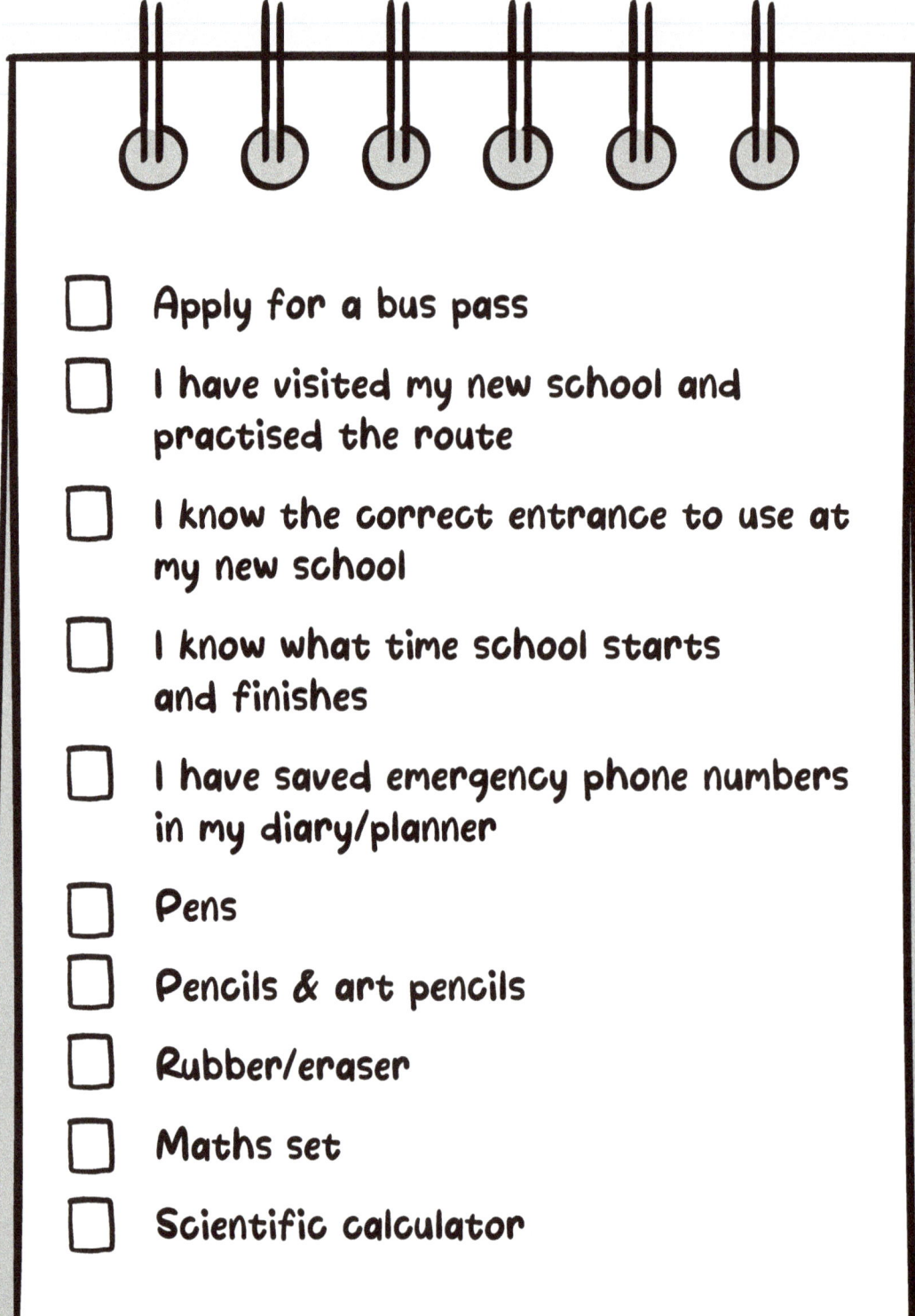

- ☐ Apply for a bus pass
- ☐ I have visited my new school and practised the route
- ☐ I know the correct entrance to use at my new school
- ☐ I know what time school starts and finishes
- ☐ I have saved emergency phone numbers in my diary/planner
- ☐ Pens
- ☐ Pencils & art pencils
- ☐ Rubber/eraser
- ☐ Maths set
- ☐ Scientific calculator

- ☐ Highlighters
- ☐ A suitable school bag for books and equipment
- ☐ I have the correct school uniform including sports/P.E kit
- ☐ Lunch money/lunch box
- ☐ Diary/planner
- ☐ Water bottle

Don't forget to pack your bag the night before!

I set a wake up alarm, otherwise, I won't wake up on time!

GOOD LUCK!

I hope you are feeling more prepared and confident about the next phase in your journey.

Get ready to create new memories, and remember to make each moment count!

Banji =)

Farewell Messages
Sign My Shirt

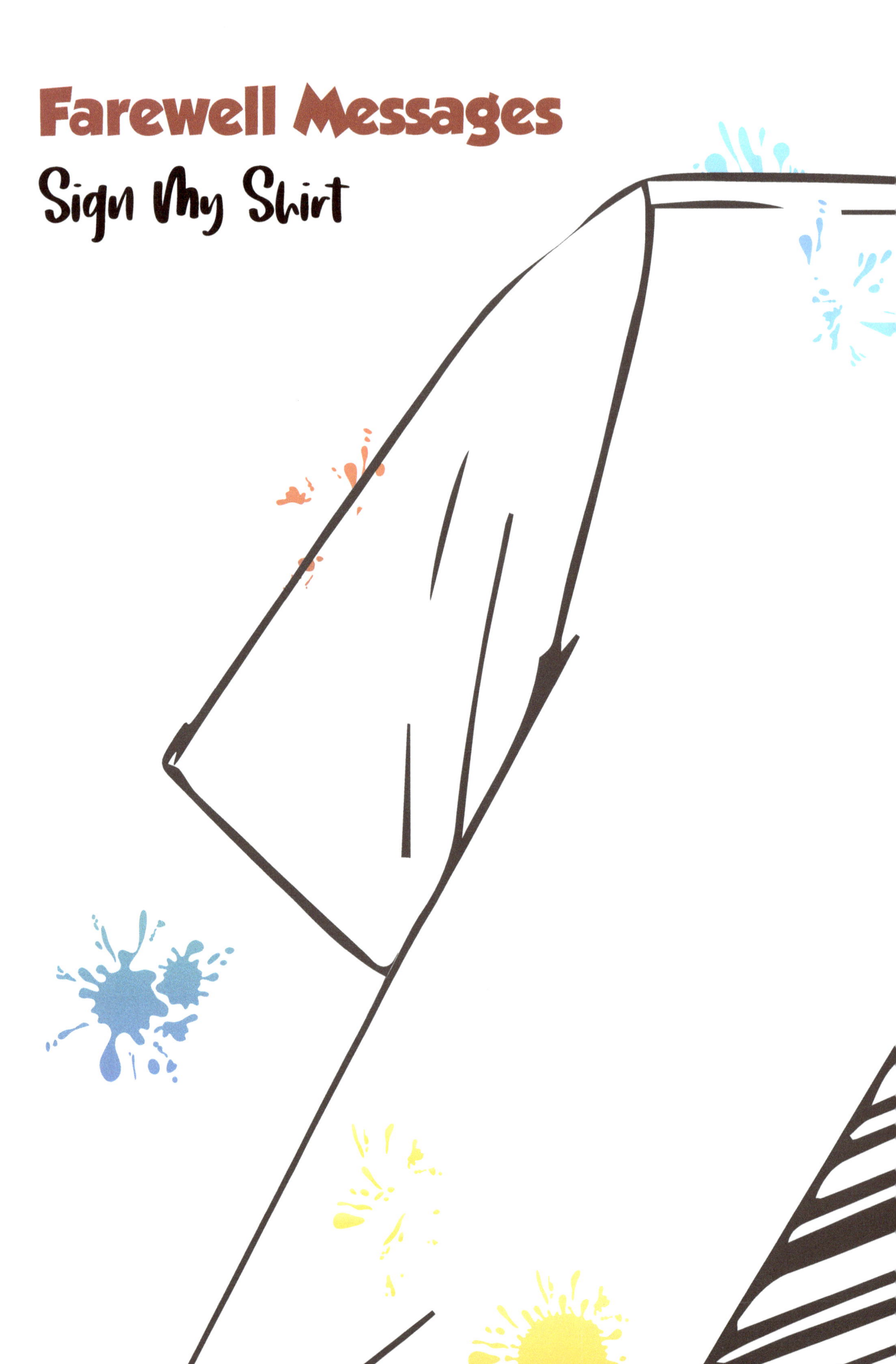

Farewell Messages
Sign My Shirt

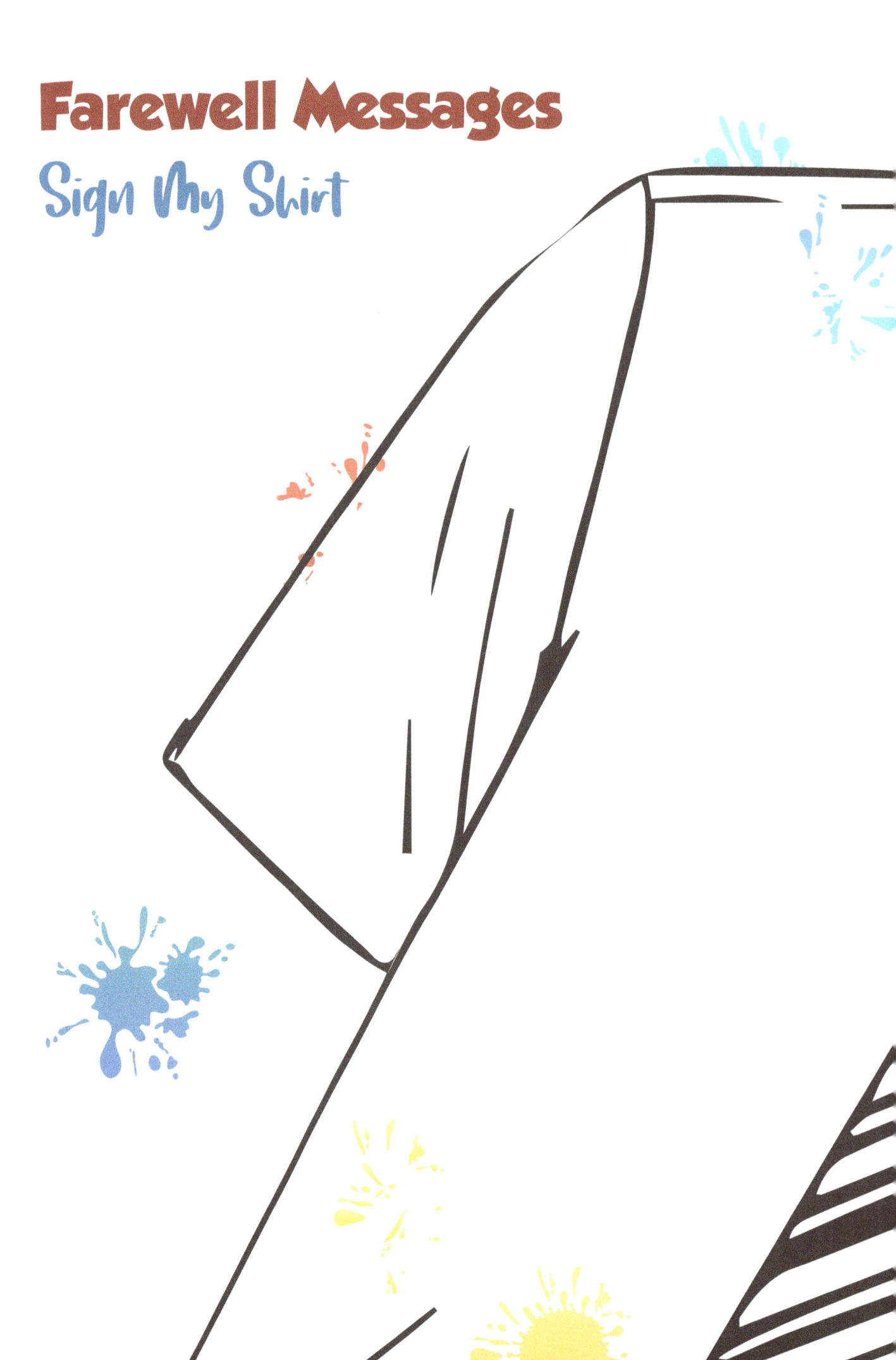

Farewell Messages
Sign My Shirt

Farewell Messages
Sign My Shirt

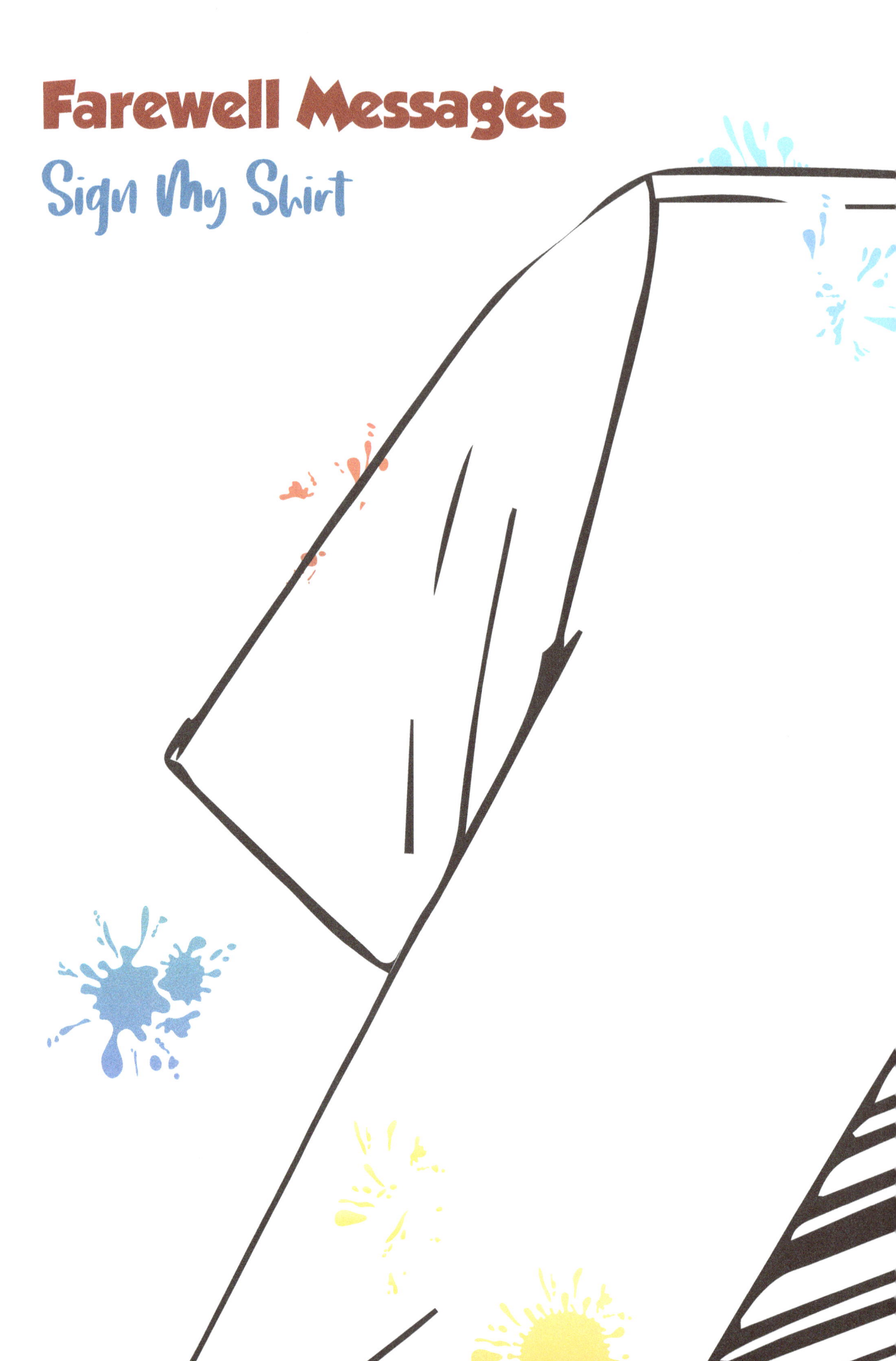

Farewell Messages
Sign My Shirt

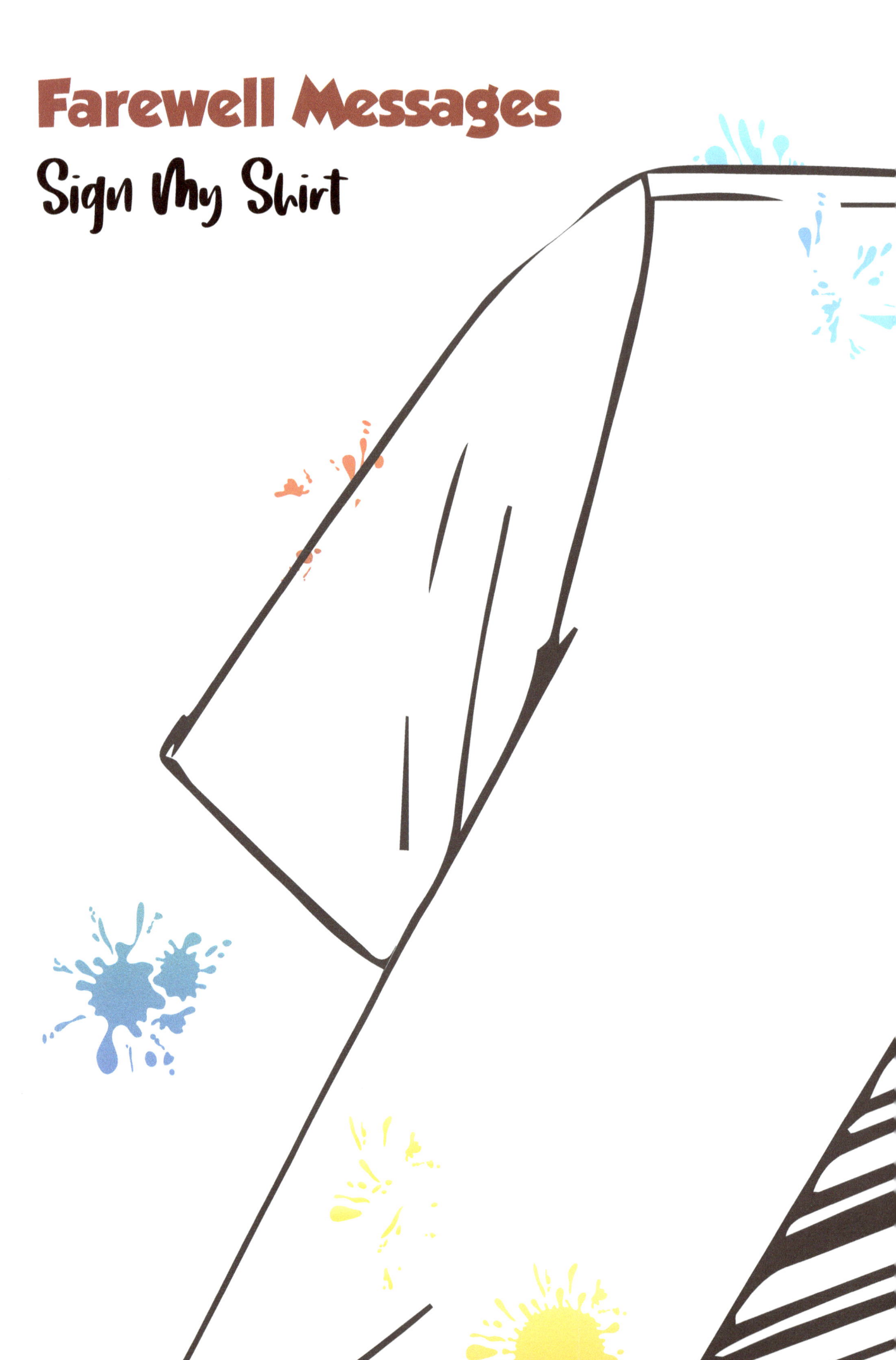

www.ingramcontent.com/pod-product-compliance
Lightning Source LLC
Chambersburg PA
CBHW040310100526
44583CB00026BA/3235